Contents

The Elf Pippo and His First Day at Work

Little elf Pippo couldn't sleep all night. It was his

big day—the first day of work at Santa Claus's workshop! He got up before dawn, put on his new green tunic, carefully stitched by his grandmother elf, and adjusted his hat on his head. "I have to do my best! Today, I'll show everyone that I'm ready

for this challenge!" he said to himself with a smile, even though a spark of r  eyes.

When Pippo entered th

The workshop was huge and full of holiday hustle and bustle. Elves were running from place to place, assembling toys, painting toy cars, and wrapping presents. Shiny machines stood on every shelf, producing beautiful dolls, plush bears, and wooden trains. Pippo felt his heart beat faster.

"Alright, Pippo!" said the chief elf, Senior Elf Timor, approaching him with a big smile. "Your first task will be to learn how to screw in bolts on mechanical toys. It's very important that everything works perfectly. Remember, every toy we create ends up in the hands of a child waiting for it."

Pippo looked at the pile of small, shiny screws and colorful toys waiting to be assembled. His hands started to tremble with excitement, but he gathered his courage and grabbed the first screw.

He tried to screw it in, but... oops! The screw slipped out of his hand, rolled across the floor, and then disappeared under one of the machines.

"Oh no!" Pippo groaned. "I messed up on my very first try."

Senior Elf Timor laughed heartily and patted Pippo on the back. "Don't worry, little elf. We all had a first day once. The most important thing is to never give up. Try again!"

Pippo took a deep breath, closed his eyes for a moment, and focused on the task. Slowly, carefully, he screwed the bolt into the toy and... he did it! The little mechanical bear came to life, waving its paw in the air. Pippo felt his heart swell with pride.

"I did it!" he shouted, his smile so wide that the other elves started clapping for him. "I did it!"

Encouraged by his first success, Pippo moved on to the next task—painting wooden toy cars. With enthusiasm, he picked up a brush and began painting the most beautiful designs he could

imagine. He painted green Christmas trees, red sleighs, and golden stars on each car, making sure each one was unique.

But in his passion for painting, Pippo didn't even notice that Santa Claus himself had come to see how the young elf was doing. As Pippo energetically waved his brush, a few drops of paint landed right on Santa's beard and suit!

The workshop fell silent. All the elves held their breath, wondering how Santa would react. But Santa Claus looked at Pippo, blinked his eyes, and then burst into laughter, his belly shaking like jelly.

"Pippo, you have the true spirit of Christmas!" Santa said, laughing heartily. "Real joy is about not being afraid to make mistakes and learning from them. I can see there's something special in you!"

Pippo blushed, but his heart was full of joy. He knew that the first day at Santa's workshop was not just about learning but also a time for friendship and discovering the magic within every elf.

As the evening came to an end, Pippo sat with Timor and the other elves by the fireplace, sipping hot chocolate with marshmallows. Christmas music softly played in the background, and all the elves laughed and shared stories about their first day at work.

"Pippo, do you know you made a great impression on Santa today?" Timor said, smiling warmly. "Your efforts and determination are exactly what make you a true Santa's elf."

"Thank you, Timor," Pippo replied, gratitude in his voice. "Today I learned that it's not just about doing everything perfectly but about never giving up and believing in yourself."

And so, little elf Pippo fell asleep that evening with a smile on his face, dreaming of all the upcoming days full of adventures that he would spend in Santa's workshop. He knew that with such support and friends by his side, he could achieve anything he dreamed of.

The Magical Reindeer on Christmas Eve

The Christmas Eve night in Lapland was frosty,

with a sky full of stars shining over the snow-covered fields. In Santa's stable, there was a buzz of excitement—the reindeer were preparing for the big holiday journey. Rudolph, Blitzen, Dancer, and the rest of the reindeer were practicing their final flights before the big takeoff, but in the corner of the stable, hidden behind a pile of hay, sat a young reindeer named Nico.

Nico was a young reindeer who had never flown before. Although he dreamed of one day leading Santa's sleigh, he was shy and full of doubts. "I can't fly as well as they can," he thought sadly, watching his older friends perform graceful aerial tricks.

Suddenly, Rudolph, the most famous of all the reindeer with his shiny, red-glowing nose, appeared in front of Nico. "Hey, Nico! What are you doing here while everyone else is practicing?" Rudolph asked with a warm smile.

"I... I'm afraid I can't do it," Nico confessed, looking down. "I can't fly like you all. I'll let Santa down if I try."

Rudolph blinked, and his nose glowed even brighter. "We all started somewhere, Nico. Even I was unsure of myself once. But you know what? I have an idea!" Rudolph said mysteriously and glanced at his friends.

In the blink of an eye, all the reindeer gathered around Nico. Blitzen, Dancer, Comet, and the rest smiled at him. "Nico, we'll help you!" they called out in unison. "We'll teach you to fly before Santa sets off on his journey!"

Before Nico could protest, the reindeer positioned him at the edge of the snow-covered field. "First, feel the magic of Christmas Eve in your heart," said Comet. "Take a deep breath and feel the joy of the season."

Nico closed his eyes and did as he was told. He took in the cool, fresh air and focused on the warm feelings of joy and hope that came with Christmas. He felt his heart beat faster, and something strange started to tingle in his hooves.

"Now, spread your wings and don't be afraid to lift off!" Blitzen encouraged him. "We're right behind you, Nico. We won't let you fall!"

Nico looked at his friends, all gazing at him with trust and belief. With a deep breath, Nico leapt off the ground... and felt his legs lift into the air! For a moment, he thought he would fall, but then Rudolph came closer and whispered, "Believe in yourself, Nico. Flying is magic, and magic begins in your heart."

And suddenly, as if the entire sky opened up before him, Nico soared higher, his hooves no longer touching the ground. The snowy field started to disappear beneath him, and for the first time in his life, he was flying! His wings—though invisible—seemed to stretch with each beat of his heart. Nico felt a sense of freedom and joy he had never experienced before.

"I'm flying! I'm really flying!" he shouted with joy, and the other reindeer began to cheer.

"We knew you could do it!" Dancer called out, spinning in the air.

At that moment, Santa Claus himself approached the reindeer, clapping his hands and smiling widely. "Nico, you did it! I knew you had the magic within you," Santa said proudly. "Tonight, you'll join us to help deliver presents to children all around the world."

Nico could hardly believe his ears. With his heart trembling with excitement, he stood alongside his older companions, ready for the greatest adventure of his life. He felt as though Christmas magic was flowing through his veins, as if every child in the world was watching him, waiting for his help.

And so, when Santa Claus called out, "Forward, reindeer! It's time to set off!" Nico lifted into the air with all his strength and confidence. He knew that with the support of his friends and belief in himself, he had discovered a magical power he never knew he had.

That night, against the sparkling sky, Nico, along with the other reindeer, brought joy and gifts to children all around the world, leaving a trail of Christmas magic behind. And from that day on, he always believed that with the help of friends and faith in himself, nothing was impossible.

The Lost Letter to Santa Claus

In a small, snow-covered town, a little girl named

Emma couldn't sleep. Christmas Eve was just around the corner, and she suddenly remembered something important—her letter to Santa Claus! Emma had written it a few days ago, carefully listing all her wishes for presents, but when she looked into her mailbox, she was horrified to discover that the letter was gone!

"Oh no! My letter to Santa is missing!" Emma cried, holding the empty envelope. Tears welled up in her eyes because she knew how much she had hoped for Santa to read her wishes.

Just then, her best friends came over: Ben, Lena, and a little dog named Max. "Don't worry, Emma!" said Ben, always ready for an adventure. "We'll find your letter together. We just need to act quickly!"

Lena looked up at the sky, where the first stars were beginning to appear. "Santa will be heading out tonight, so we have to find the letter before he arrives in town!" she said with determination.

All four of them—Emma, Ben, Lena, and Max—set off through the snow-covered streets of the town. They started their search at the mailbox in the Main Square, where Emma had last seen her letter. Max sniffed the snow, trying to pick up any scent.

Suddenly, Max started barking happily and wagging his tail, pointing to tiny paw prints in the snow. "It must be a squirrel! Maybe it took your letter, thinking it was something tasty to eat!" Ben said, his eyes lighting up.

Following the tracks, the children reached a big, old oak tree where a squirrel named Cinnamon lived. The branches were decorated with lots of small nuts and holiday ornaments. Cinnamon peeked out from his hollow and smiled at the kids.

"Cinnamon, have you seen a letter to Santa Claus by any chance?" Lena asked, waving to the squirrel.

The squirrel blinked his big eyes and pointed to a branch where Emma's pink letter was hanging, with a hazelnut stuck to it. "Oh, I'm sorry! I thought it was something to eat!" Cinnamon said apologetically.

"Thank you, Cinnamon! It's really important!" Emma said, taking the letter and hugging it close to her chest. "But now we still need to get it to Santa in time!"

The kids knew that Santa might soon be flying over the town, so they ran quickly to the hilltop that overlooked the entire area. When they reached the top, they saw a red glow in the sky—it was Rudolph's nose lighting the way for Santa!

Emma, trembling with excitement, waved the letter above her head. "Santa! Santa!" she called out as loudly as she could. At that moment, Santa slowed his sleigh and looked down to where the children were waving on the hill.

Santa descended a little lower and gave a big smile. "Emma, I heard you had a little trouble with your letter," he said warmly. "But I see that thanks to your friends, you managed to find it!"

Emma, happy and moved, handed the letter to Santa. "Yes, Santa. My friends helped me find the letter, and now I can make my biggest Christmas wish come true."

Santa looked at Ben, Lena, and Max, then winked at Emma. "This is the true spirit of Christmas— helping, friendship, and working together. Your hearts are full of magic!" he said. "And now, Emma, I promise that your letters will always reach me, no matter where they get lost."

As Santa's sleigh lifted back into the sky, the children stood on the hill, waving goodbye with their hearts full of joy and hope. Emma knew that even if something gets lost sometimes, true friends will always help find what matters most.

And so, Christmas Eve became even more magical thanks to the adventure of the lost letter, and Emma learned that the real magic of Christmas isn't just about presents but the power of friendship and shared joy.

The Chocolate Adventure on the Christmas Tree

On Christmas Eve, while all the children in the town were fast asleep, something extraordinary was happening in the Williams family's house. A big, beautifully decorated Christmas tree stood in the living room, its branches sparkling with colorful ornaments, lights, and... chocolate decorations. Chocolate Santas, reindeer, and snowflakes hung from the branches, waiting for the children to discover them the next morning. But that night, something incredible was about to happen.

As the clock struck midnight, something strange began to occur. A small chocolate Santa, hanging on the lowest branch, suddenly opened his eyes and looked around. "Can this be? I'm alive!" he exclaimed in amazement, staring at his chocolate hands.

Next to him, a chocolate reindeer shook its head and joyfully realized it had come to life too. "This is amazing! I've always dreamed of seeing the world from up high! Hey, Santa, let's climb to the top of the tree!" the reindeer shouted with excitement.

Soon, all the chocolate decorations started to move. Tiny chocolate snowflakes began dancing on the branches, and chocolate stars glittered in the light of the tree. There were even a few chocolate snowmen who laughed and rolled around as they tumbled from the lower branches onto the soft cotton snow at the base of the tree.

"Wait for me!" called the chocolate Santa as he climbed higher up the branches. "We have to reach the very top before dawn when the children find us!"

The chocolate ornaments eagerly started their climb, laughing and helping each other along the way. Every step up was filled with joy and holiday spirit. The chocolate reindeer bounced from branch to branch, shouting, "We're getting closer! We'll see the world from the highest point!"

At one point, a chocolate snowflake, climbing up a delicate twig, wobbled and began to fall! "Oh no!" she cried out, but the chocolate Santa quickly caught her and pulled her close.

"Don't worry, little snowflake! We'll do this together!" Santa said with a warm smile. "During Christmas, we always help each other."

When they finally reached the top of the tree, all the chocolate decorations paused for a moment and looked down. The view was breathtaking! The entire living room glowed in the light of the tree, and in the distance, through the window, they could see the snow-covered town. Chocolate Santa looked up and saw the star at the top of the tree.

"Look how beautiful it is! We've made it to the very top!" he shouted with joy. "This is the best adventure I've ever had!"

At that moment, the chocolate reindeer, watching the snowflakes dance around the star, said, "I wish every Christmas Eve could be this magical. Together, we can achieve anything!"

Suddenly, the clock struck one, and the chocolate decorations began to feel themselves hardening. Their Christmas adventure was coming to an end. Each one returned to its place on the branches, smiling at each other with joy in their eyes.

"See you next year, my friends," whispered the chocolate Santa, closing his eyes.

When morning came, the children ran into the living room with sparkling eyes, discovering the chocolate decorations on the tree. "Mom, Dad, look! Chocolate Santas and reindeer!" they shouted, reaching for the sweet treats.

A little boy, looking at the chocolate Santa at the top of the tree, quietly said, "You know what, Mom? I think these chocolate ornaments have a little bit of magic in them. I think they had an adventure last night!"

Mom smiled mysteriously and replied, "You know, son, on Christmas Eve, anything is possible. Maybe they really did come to life for a moment to see the world from up high."

And even though the children never knew about the adventure of the chocolate decorations, the magic of Christmas filled the air, making every heart overflow with joy and the spirit of the holiday.

The Snowflakes That Grant Wishes

In a small, picturesque town surrounded by dense forests and snow-covered hills, the children couldn't wait for Christmas Eve. Everyone knew that it was a night when the most wonderful things happened. Legends said that during the first snowfall on Christmas Eve, every snowflake held the magical power to grant wishes. The children in the town believed that if you caught one of those snowflakes and made a wish from your heart, it would surely come true.

Little Anna and her brother John sat by the window, gazing up at the sky. It was almost midnight, and everything was quiet. The snow hadn't started falling yet, but there was a sense of magic and anticipation in the air.

"Do you think the snowflakes will really grant wishes this year?" John asked, trying to hide his impatience.

Anna smiled at her brother. "I believe they will, John. But we have to remember that our wishes must be truly important and come straight from the heart."

Just then, something magical began to happen. The first snowflakes appeared in the sky, falling faster and faster, creating a swirling dance of white stars. Anna and John rushed outside, holding their hands out to the sky, trying to catch their magical snowflakes.

Anna was the first to catch a snowflake. She held it gently in her hand, and her face lit up with a broad smile. "My wish is for Olivia, my best friend, to get the dress she's been dreaming of," she whispered, watching as the snowflake slowly melted in her warm hands.

John caught his snowflake a moment later. He closed his eyes and thought for a while. "I wish for a new soccer ball!" he said with hope in his voice, and his snowflake also disappeared, as if it had absorbed his wish.

Soon, other children from the town joined them in the yard, each with a wish on their lips. One child, little Jasio, wished for his family to have a full table for the Christmas dinner, while Malgosia hoped that her grandfather would get well soon.

After sharing their wishes, the children returned to their homes, filled with hope and anticipation.

But what happened the next morning was more than they could have imagined.

When Anna woke up on Christmas morning, she ran outside to see if her snowflake had brought any surprises. To her amazement, there was Olivia, wearing the most beautiful red dress she had ever dreamed of! "Anna! Look at this!" Olivia exclaimed with joy, twirling around as the dress sparkled in the winter sunlight. "This is the most wonderful gift I could ever wish for! How did this happen?"

Anna smiled and said, "It's the magic of the snowflakes, Olivia. Sometimes, our dreams come true when we truly believe in them."

John, while happy for Olivia's joy, couldn't help but feel a little sad. His wish for a new soccer ball hadn't come true the way he imagined. But just then, he saw little Jasio running toward him with a huge smile on his face.

"John! Look!" Jasio called, showing a large basket filled with food that his family found at their doorstep. "We have a full table for Christmas dinner! Thanks to your wish, John!"

John looked at Jasio in disbelief. "Me? That wasn't my wish, Jasio..." he began, but then he understood. Snowflakes don't always grant wishes the way we expect. Sometimes, they bring joy to others in ways we never imagined.

Suddenly, as everyone stood together in the town square, the last, most beautiful snowflake of the night fell on John. He caught it in his hands and felt a warmth spreading through his fingers. And right beside him, in the snow, lay a perfectly shiny new soccer ball—exactly the one he had wished for.

"See, Anna?" he said with a smile. "The snowflakes really do have magic. And the best gift is that we can share that magic with others."

The children in the town learned that the true magic of Christmas wasn't in what they received, but in the joy they could give to others. And though each snowflake had only one wish to grant, its magic was in making sure that when our wishes are for others, kindness always comes back to us in the most unexpected ways.

That Christmas Eve in the town was not only white and wintry but also filled with love, friendship, and the warmth of the holiday spirit. The children knew that the magic of the snowflakes didn't end with the new year but lasted all year long in the hearts of those who believed in the miraculous power of giving.

Santa's Riddle

On the day before Christmas Eve, as Santa Claus

and his elves were finishing the preparations for the big holiday journey, something completely unexpected happened. In the middle of the workshop, among piles of wrapped gifts and the sound of jingling bells, a mysterious card appeared. It was red with green patterns, and in the center was a message: "Dear Santa, a special surprise awaits you. Solve the riddles, and you will find out who prepared it."

Santa raised his eyebrows in surprise and looked at his elves, who also stopped working, staring at the card with curiosity. "Well, well, it looks like someone wants to test me!" Santa said with a smile, scratching his beard. "Elves, are you ready for an adventure?"

The elves cheered enthusiastically, jumping up and down with excitement. Their little faces lit up in anticipation of a journey filled with mysteries and holiday surprises. Senior Elf Timor, who was always ready for action, read the first riddle out loud:

"You'll find me where the toys are hidden, where all the parts lie neatly bidden. Hammers, screws, and paints all gleam, this is where the elves always teem."

"The toy workshop!" one of the younger elves shouted. "It must be our workshop!"

Santa and the elves rushed to the largest workshop, where all the presents were being made. There, between shelves filled with tools, they found another card, decorated with silver stars. This time the riddle read:

"In the place where cookies bake in the oven, where cinnamon and gingerbread dream of lovin'. Sweet scents rise up in the air, this is where the next clue will pair."

"The elves' kitchen!" Santa said, licking his lips at the thought of gingerbread.

In the elves' kitchen, the smell of freshly baked cookies and hot chocolate filled the air. There, on the table, they found another card with a riddle. This one, however, was a bit more challenging:

"I am closest to the stars, where the sky shines bright, where reindeer lift you up, all snug and tight. You'll find me among snow and breeze, where it's always magical, with such ease."

Santa looked at his reindeer and knew that it must be the reindeer stables. When they arrived there, they saw Rudolph and the other reindeer watching them with interest. Attached to Rudolph's antlers was another card, the last riddle of their adventure.

"You'll find me where the heart of Christmas beats, where all wishes come true in discreet. Where the Christmas tree's star shines high, and joy fills every heart that sighs."

Santa smiled widely. "It must be the Grand Christmas Tree in the village center!" he exclaimed.

When everyone reached the tree, they saw a large box wrapped in a golden ribbon. Santa untied the ribbon and opened the lid. Inside were hundreds of small gifts, along with a big card that said: "Thank you, Santa, for all the joy and love you bring. These gifts are from us—your elves, as a token of our gratitude!"

Santa was so touched that his eyes glistened with tears. "My dear friends!" he said, hugging the elves. "This is the most beautiful gift I could have ever wished for. I always thought I was the one spreading joy, but now I see that the true magic of Christmas is when we all share love and kindness."

The elves jumped with joy, knowing that their plan had worked. Together, they danced around the Christmas tree, singing holiday songs and laughing with delight. Santa thanked each of the elves for their hard work and support, which make Christmas so special every year.

And so, on that magical evening, Santa Claus discovered that the most precious gifts aren't toys and decorations but love, friendship, and the shared joy that make the holidays truly magical.

The Christmas Tree in the Heart of the Town

In a dense, old forest, where the trees grew tall

and majestic, there stood a small, green fir tree named Lusia. Lusia wasn't the biggest or the most impressive tree in the forest, but she had one big dream: she wanted to become the town's Christmas tree, decorated with the most beautiful lights and ornaments that would light up the hearts of everyone in the town.

Every year, Lusia watched as the foresters chose a tree to stand in the town square. They always picked the biggest and straightest trees, and Lusia felt that her dream was too far away. "Will I ever be big enough to become the town's Christmas tree?" she wondered sadly.

One frosty winter, as Christmas Eve was fast approaching, the important moment arrived. The town workers came to the forest to choose a tree for the holiday display. Lusia knew this was her only chance. She stood up as straight as she could, trying to look bigger and more majestic.

"Look at that tree!" one of the workers exclaimed, pointing at Lusia. "It's not the biggest, but there's something special about it. It has the perfect shape of a Christmas tree, as if it wants to light up the whole square with its charm."

"That's true!" agreed another worker. "It has the spirit of Christmas. Let's take it to the town square!"

Lusia couldn't believe her ears! Her dream was coming true! She was carefully lifted onto a large truck and carried through the forest, past fields and houses, until they reached the heart of the town, where she was placed in the center of the main square. The townspeople gathered around, looking in awe at their new Christmas tree.

The workers began decorating Lusia with colorful lights, golden ribbons, and beautiful ornaments. Every branch was adorned in such a way that Lusia shone like never before. As night fell, the townspeople gathered around the square, holding hands and singing carols. Children danced around the tree, their laughter filling the air.

Finally, the moment of truth arrived. The town's mayor stepped onto a small stage next to Lusia and announced, "People of our town! It's time for our new Christmas tree to light up the hearts of everyone here. Ready? Three, two, one!"

At that very moment, as all the lights on Lusia lit up, the entire square glowed with thousands of colorful lights. They illuminated the faces of the people, reflecting in their eyes full of wonder and joy. Lusia felt her heart swell with happiness—her dream had finally come true!

"I'm here to bring joy to everyone who looks at me!" Lusia thought, watching the townspeople celebrate around her. "This is the moment I've grown for."

Beneath her branches, little children began exchanging gifts and sharing holiday stories. People sang carols, danced, and reveled in the magic of the evening. Everyone knew that this was the most beautiful Christmas tree they had ever had, not just because of its appearance but because it held something more—the spirit of dreams and holiday magic.

As the night turned into a chilly dawn, Lusia stood proudly in the square, looking over the town that was drifting off to sleep after the festive celebration. She knew that she had fulfilled her greatest wish—she had brought joy and the warmth of the holiday spirit to everyone in the town.

And although the coming years might bring new Christmas trees to the town square, the townspeople would always remember that special night when a little fir tree with big dreams lit up the hearts of the whole town.

Bob the Bear's Christmas Eve Journey

In the heart of the snowy forest lived a bear named Bob. He was a bear with a big heart, always ready to help his friends. On Christmas Eve, as the forest was covered with a blanket of white snow and the stars shone brighter than usual, Bob decided to set off on a special mission.

Bob had a little friend, a squirrel named Sophia, who dreamed of having the most beautiful ornament in the world. Every year, Sophia decorated her tree in the middle of the forest, but she always felt it was missing that one special ornament that would make her Christmas tree truly magical.

"I must find something special for Sophia," Bob said to himself, wrapping his warm scarf around his neck as he set off. "I promised her that this Christmas Eve would be unforgettable!"

Bob trudged through the forest, the snow crunching under his paws. Along the way, he met Asher the fox, who was digging in the snow, looking for nuts. "Hey, Asher!" Bob called out. "Do you know where I can find the biggest and most beautiful ornament for Sophia?"

Asher thought for a moment, then waved his tail. "I've heard that near Lake Rosa, the most beautiful ice crystals shine. Maybe you'll find something there that looks like an ornament."

Bob thanked Asher and headed toward the lake. When he arrived, he saw an incredible sight—the entire lake was covered in ice crystals that sparkled like diamonds in the moonlight. But despite their beauty, Bob knew they weren't the ornaments he was looking for.

"I have to keep searching," he said to himself with determination.

As Bob continued his journey through the forest, he met Lucas the hedgehog, who was known for his love of holiday decorations. "Lucas, can you help me?" Bob asked. "I'm looking for an ornament for Sophia, something truly special."

Lucas the hedgehog smiled and pointed to the tall pine trees. "At the top of the tallest pine tree grows a unique fruit—red as a ruby. Maybe it could be a beautiful ornament for Sophia."

With hope in his heart, Bob climbed the tree, but when he reached the fruit, he realized that even though it was lovely, it wasn't what he was looking for. Disappointed, he climbed back down, but he didn't lose hope.

Finally, he met Emma the owl, who was perched on a branch, gazing at the night sky. "Emma, could you help me find the biggest and most beautiful ornament in the world?" Bob asked.

Emma the owl smiled mysteriously and replied, "The most beautiful ornaments aren't always what we see on the outside, but what they hold in their glow. Sometimes, you have to look at something ordinary and see the magic in it."

Bob thanked Emma for her wise words but felt a little confused. He wondered what the owl could have meant. As he walked home, feeling a bit discouraged, he noticed something incredible. On one of the small trees, completely covered in snow, hung a tiny, transparent drop of ice. In the moonlight, the ice glistened with a thousand colors, as if it held the magic of Christmas Eve itself.

Bob carefully took the ice from the branch and smiled wide. "This is it! This is the ornament I've been looking for! It has all the magic Sophia dreamed of."

When he returned to Sophia and showed her the icy gem, the little squirrel was speechless with amazement. "Bob! This is the most beautiful ornament I've ever seen!" Sophia exclaimed, jumping with joy.

Together, they hung the icy gem at the top of the tree. As the lights began to twinkle, the ornament reflected their glow, casting colorful reflections all over the tree. The entire forest seemed to shine and pulse with the magic of that special night.

"Emma was right," Bob thought. "The most beautiful things aren't the ones we can buy, but those we discover when we look with our hearts."

And so, that Christmas Eve became even more special because Bob realized that true magic doesn't lie in perfect objects but in the love and friendship we share with others.

The Little Angel on the Top of the Christmas Tree

In a distant, magical land where snow never melted and stars shone the brightest, there was a factory of angels getting ready for Christmas. Every year, from this factory, little angels were sent out to take their place at the tops of Christmas trees all around the world. This year, one of the angels chosen for this special task was a tiny angel named Aurelius.

Aurelius was one of the youngest angels in the factory. He had wings as delicate as snowflakes and a halo that twinkled like a star, but he had one big problem—he was afraid of heights. While all the other angels eagerly awaited their moment to sit at the top of the tree and shine, Aurelius trembled at the thought of climbing to the highest branches.

"What's wrong, Aurelius?" asked an older angel named Seraphina, who noticed the sadness in the little angel's eyes. "Why aren't you as excited as the rest of us?"

Aurelius looked down and said quietly, "I'm afraid I won't be able to do it. Everyone's waiting for me to sit on top of the tree, but what if I slip, fall, and ruin the whole celebration?"

Seraphina smiled warmly and wrapped her wings around Aurelius. "We all get scared sometimes, especially when we have to do something difficult," she said. "But remember, the magic of Christmas is inside all of us. The most important thing is to believe in yourself and let others support you."

That evening, as night fell and Christmas lights began to twinkle in the homes, Aurelius was taken to the town square, where the biggest Christmas tree in the whole land stood. People had gathered to celebrate, and at the very top of this enormous tree was a spot reserved just for him.

Aurelius looked up and felt his heart race. The tree was so tall that its top seemed to touch the clouds! "I can't do it," he thought in panic, but before he could back away, the other angels gathered around him.

"Don't worry, Aurelius!" called out a small angel named Florian, holding his hand. "We're all here to help you!"

All the angels began to flap their wings, creating a swirl of magical dust that gently lifted Aurelius into the air. He felt his heart begin to calm, and his fear was slowly replaced by excitement. He flew higher and higher, and with each flap of his wings, he came closer to the top of the tree.

When he finally reached the top, he was surrounded by the glow of the stars and the twinkling lights of the tree. The whole square lit up with joy, and the people looked up, gazing at Aurelius in awe. A wide smile spread across his face, and a spark of courage flickered in his eyes, something he had never felt before.

"See?" Seraphina called out to all the angels. "Aurelius not only overcame his fear but made the whole tree shine brighter than ever!"

The people in the square began to cheer, and the children sang carols, looking up at the little angel on the top of the tree, who now lit up the entire area. Aurelius felt his heart fill with the warmth and love of the holiday spirit.

"It's true that sometimes we're afraid of heights," he thought, looking at the stars above him. "But when we have friends and support around us, we can achieve anything."

And so, the little angel Aurelius discovered that his courage had been within him all along—all he needed was to believe in himself and trust the magic of Christmas, which lifted him high up into the sky.

The Mystery of the Christmas Cake

In a small town where Christmas lights twinkled on every street, there lived a little baker named Max. Max loved baking cakes, gingerbread, and cupcakes, but he dreamed of creating something truly special for Christmas Eve—a cake that would taste as magical as the holiday itself.

One frosty evening, while Max was searching through his grandmother's attic, he stumbled upon an old, dusty cookbook. On its cover were the words: "Recipes of the Christmas Wizards." Max opened the book, and his eyes lit up as he found a recipe for a "Magical Christmas Wish-Granting Cake."

"This cake grants the wish of anyone who tastes it!" Max read aloud, hardly believing his eyes. But then he noticed a small note written in tiny handwriting at the bottom of the page: "Warning! The cake only works if it's baked with heart and joy."

Max decided that he would bake this magical cake for Christmas Eve and take it to the town's holiday festival. He began gathering all the necessary ingredients: flour, eggs, sugar, spices, and a pinch of festive cinnamon. But as he mixed the ingredients, he felt that something was missing. The cake didn't smell as delightful as he imagined it would.

"What am I doing wrong?" Max wondered, looking over the recipe once more. He knew the key to success was baking with heart and joy, but he just didn't feel the magic he was hoping to capture.

Just then, a group of children from the town burst into the kitchen: Little Emma, Willy, and Lena, all with smiles on their faces and laughter filling the air. "Max! We heard you're baking something special! Can we help you?" Emma asked, bouncing with excitement.

Max looked at the children and realized that this was what he was missing—joy, shared laughter, and the spirit of Christmas. "Of course! I need your help to make this cake truly magical," he said with a big smile.

The children began to mix the ingredients, adding holiday spices to the cake and singing Christmas carols, while Max felt warmth growing in his heart. Together, they danced around the oven, their laughter echoing throughout the house. The cake turned a golden color, and its scent filled the kitchen and the entire neighborhood.

When the cake was ready, Max and the children carried it to the town square, where everyone had gathered for the holiday festival. With a slight tremble in his heart, Max cut the first slice and gave it to an elderly lady who had always wished to visit her grandchildren in a faraway country.

The lady took a bite of the cake, closed her eyes, and suddenly felt warmth spread through her heart. "Max, this cake is amazing!" she said, tears welling up in her eyes. "I just received a message that my grandchildren are coming home for Christmas!"

People began to line up, each holding a little wish in their hearts. As soon as they tasted the magical cake, their faces lit up, and smiles spread wide across their faces. Max watched as everyone who tried his creation received what they wished for—not always in a literal way, but always in a way that filled their hearts with joy.

"It's true that the secret of this cake lies in heart and joy," Max thought, seeing the happiness spread through the square. "The best ingredients are love, laughter, and shared fun."

As the evening came to an end, Max stood in the square with the children, looking up at the starry sky. He knew that something more than just the townspeople's wishes had come true that Christmas Eve—his own dream of sharing the warmth and magic of the holiday with others had come true.

And so, Max's magical Christmas cake became a legend in the town, and everyone knew that its secret wasn't in the exotic ingredients, but in the heart and joy that went into making it.

Santa's Lost Hat

In Santa's workshop, nestled in the heart of

Lapland, there was a flurry of activity. Elves were rushing about, packing the last of the presents and checking the wish lists of children from all around the world. Everything was almost ready for the big Christmas journey when suddenly, a distressed voice echoed through the workshop.

"Oh no! Where's my hat?" Santa Claus called out, searching through his pockets and staring in disbelief at the empty shelf where his beloved red hat with the white pompom usually sat.

The elves immediately stopped in their tracks, and the workshop fell silent. Without his hat, Santa couldn't start his journey! The hat was not only a symbol of Christmas but also brought him luck and gave him the magical power to deliver presents on time.

Senior Elf Timor looked at his team of elves and shouted, "Elves, we need to act fast! We must find Santa's hat before he sets off! Everyone, take your positions and search every corner of the workshop!"

The elves sprang into action. They darted around the workshop, looking under tables, rummaging through boxes of decorations, and checking bags full of gifts. The smallest elf in the whole workshop, named Felix, was running with even more determination than the others. Though he was the youngest and smallest, he always dreamed of doing something truly important for Santa Claus.

"Don't worry, Santa! I'll find your hat!" Felix called out, his voice barely audible over the hustle and bustle of the workshop.

Felix searched in every possible place until finally, when he peeked behind a large pile of colorful ribbons, he saw something red sticking out from under a festive rug. He quickly ran over, lifted the corner of the rug, and there it was—Santa's lost hat!

With a broad smile and a heart full of pride, Felix grabbed the hat and dashed over to Santa. "I found it! I found your hat!" he shouted, jumping up and down with joy.

Santa Claus looked at Felix with a huge grin. "Felix, you're a real hero!" he said, putting the hat back on his head. "Without you, I wouldn't be able to start my Christmas journey. You saved Christmas!"

All the elves cheered, and little Felix felt like the biggest elf in the whole workshop. He had never been prouder of his achievement. Santa walked over to him and shook his hand, saying, "Thanks to you, Felix, children all around the world will receive their presents on time. You have a heart bigger than anyone else!"

As Santa's sleigh finally took off into the sky and the reindeer charged forward, Felix looked up at the night sky, full of joy and satisfaction. He knew that because of his small act, the magic of Christmas would reach homes all around the world that night.

And so, Felix, the smallest elf in the workshop, became the hero of that special Christmas Eve. When everyone returned to the workshop after the journey, Santa presented Felix with a special reward—a small, golden star to wear on his own hat, as a symbol of courage and dedication.

From that day on, Felix was not only the smallest but also one of the most respected elves in the entire workshop. And everyone knew that no matter your size, you can be a hero if you put your heart and dedication into everything you do.

The Christmas Party for All the Animals

Deep in the heart of the snow-covered forest, where the trees stood like white sentinels, the animals were preparing for their annual Christmas Party. It was the most important night of the year when all the woodland creatures—from the tiniest ants to the biggest bears—gathered together to celebrate the magic of Christmas.

This year, the main organizers of the party were Olivia the squirrel and her best friend, Janek the hedgehog. "We have to prepare something truly special!" said Olivia, gathering nuts and seeds for the holiday feast. "This party has to be the best one ever!"

Janek nodded and began rolling apples into a small basket. "We have to remember that everyone in the forest brings something to share," he said, smiling. "It's not just about the food, but about being together."

As evening approached, the animals began to gather at the clearing, where a festive table was set up on a large tree stump. There were plenty of treats: dried berries brought by the rabbits, nuts and seeds collected by the squirrels, the freshest apples from the hedgehogs, and delicious honey from the bees.

Everyone was very excited until suddenly, they noticed that Lucas the fox was sitting alone at the edge of the clearing, looking sadly at his friends. "Lucas, what's wrong?" asked Olivia, walking up to him. "Why aren't you joining us?"

"I have nothing to share at the party," Lucas replied, looking down. "Everything I had froze in my pantry. I couldn't find any food because of this cold winter."

Olivia looked at Janek, and they exchanged knowing smiles. "That doesn't matter, Lucas!" Olivia exclaimed. "Christmas isn't just about sharing food; it's about sharing your heart and time with friends. Come on, sit with us! You're more than welcome here."

Then, all the animals began to gather around Lucas. Elijah the rabbit brought him a handful of dried berries, and Janek the hedgehog offered him his tastiest apple. "Friendship is the most important ingredient of Christmas," said Janek. "Sometimes, just being together is enough."

Lucas looked at his friends and felt his heart fill with warmth. Even though he didn't bring any food, he knew he was part of something bigger—a community where everyone cared for one another.

As the night deepened, snow began to gently fall, creating a white blanket on the clearing. The animals danced around the Christmas tree, sang songs, and shared stories of their adventures. The little mice danced with the squirrels, and James the bear laughed so loudly that the echo of his laughter carried through the whole forest.

Suddenly, a magical star that woodpecker Levi had brought lit up in the center of the table. "This is a special gift for everyone," said Levi, placing the star on top of the Christmas tree. "Let this star remind us how important friendship, cooperation, and sharing are, especially in the toughest times."

As the star lit up the entire clearing, the animals looked at each other with smiles on their faces. They realized that it wasn't the food or the presents that created the magic of Christmas but the love, support, and the fact that they were all together—no matter what.

"This was the best Christmas in our forest," said Lucas the fox, smiling at his friends. "Thank you for reminding me what truly matters."

And so, as the night of Christmas Eve came to an end, the animals settled down in their warm burrows and nests, knowing that the real treasure of the holiday was their friendship. And in each of their hearts remained the hope that next year, they would meet again in the clearing to celebrate what was most important—together.

The Little Star and Her Wish

High in the sky, where the winter night stretched

out like a vast canvas, lived a tiny star named Stella. Stella was one of the smallest stars in the sky, barely visible among her bigger and brighter companions. Though she was small, she had a big dream—to be the brightest star in the sky on Christmas Eve, to light the way for Santa Claus and bring joy to all the children around the world.

Every night, Stella would look up at her bigger sisters, shining like diamonds. "I wish I could be as bright and beautiful as they are," she said with a sigh. "But how can a little star like me light up the whole sky?"

Stella had a friend, a large and wise star named Polaris, known as the North Star, who always shone the brightest. One night, when Stella felt the most discouraged, Polaris looked at her and gave a warm smile.

"Why are you so sad, little Stella?" Polaris asked.

"Oh, Polaris, you always shine so brightly, and I barely twinkle among the other stars," Stella replied, looking down. "I wish I could be like you. I want to light up the sky on Christmas Eve and bring people hope."

Polaris thought for a moment, then said, "You know, Stella, brightness doesn't just come from our glow on the outside. True light comes from the heart, from believing in yourself, and from what we can give to others. Christmas Eve is full of magic, and you have more power inside you than you think."

Stella wanted to believe Polaris's words, but she still felt small and weak. However, she decided that she would do everything in her power to shine her brightest on that special night.

When Christmas Eve finally arrived, Stella took a deep breath and focused all her energy, trying to glow as brightly as she could. For a moment, her light seemed to grow stronger, but then it faded, and Stella fell back, feeling exhausted. "I can't do it," she whispered to herself. "I'll never be as bright as the other stars."

Suddenly, something extraordinary began to happen on the ground below. Children from a small town, waiting for Santa Claus to arrive, looked up at the sky and noticed the tiny star flickering with all its might. A little girl named Ania pointed at Stella and said, "Look! That little star is trying so hard to shine just for us!"

The children started singing Christmas carols, looking at Stella with such joy that warmth filled her heart. She realized that it wasn't her size or strength that made her important but her desire to bring light and hope to others.

"I will shine for them," Stella thought. "For those who need a little bit of hope and love on this magical night."

In that moment, Stella began to shine brighter than ever before. Her light was warm and full of love, and it reached every corner of the town. Even Santa Claus, flying through the night sky in his sleigh, looked up at the little star and smiled broadly.

"Thank you, Stella," Santa said, waving to her from above. "Thanks to your light, I will always find my way to the children who are waiting for my presents."

Stella felt her heart swell with pride and joy. Polaris looked at her and said, "See, Stella? Your light came from your heart. You are the brightest star because you shine with love and faith in what you can give to others."

From that night on, Stella understood that you don't have to be the biggest or the brightest star in the sky to make a difference. True brightness comes from the heart, from how much you want to shine for others.

And so, every Christmas Eve, when children look up at the sky and see a little twinkling star, they know it's Stella—the little star who learned that her light has the power to bring hope to everyone who gazes upon her.

Christmas Eve of the Toys

In a quiet, cozy room, where the Christmas tree glowed with lights and the presents were neatly arranged beneath its branches, stood the toys— silent and still, as if waiting for something magical. It was Christmas Eve, the most special night of the year when something extraordinary always happened. As the last lights in the house went out and the children fell asleep in their beds, something began to stir.

One by one, the toys started to come to life. A plush bear named Charles stretched and yawned, waking up Sarah the doll, who began smoothing out her dress. The little wooden soldier, David, stood at attention, and the toy car, Mark, began to spin its wheels, ready for action.

"Hello, friends!" called Charles, looking around the room. "It's our magical night! We only have one night a year to come alive and have our Christmas celebration!"

"But we must also remember that Santa Claus will come to check if everything is ready for the children!" added Sarah, bouncing on her tiny feet. "We need to make sure the presents are beautifully wrapped and prepared for delivery."

The toys set to work with incredible enthusiasm. Charles began sorting the presents, arranging them in neat piles, while Sarah decorated them with ribbons and colorful bows. The wooden soldier, David, stood guard, making sure no presents went missing.

"Hey, Mark! Check to see if the path to the chimney is clear and ready for Santa's arrival!" called Charles. Mark zoomed toward the fireplace, racing up and down the rug, making sure the way was safe and free of obstacles.

Suddenly, the sound of a bell echoed through the room, signaling something important. It was Jessica the plush owl, who flew in through the window and perched on the Christmas tree. "I have news from the North Pole!" Jessica announced, flapping her wings. "Santa Claus is getting close! We need to hurry!"

The toys started working even faster, organizing their Christmas party. Sarah set up little twinkling lights around the tree, and Charles brought out cookies and milk to leave for Santa. Together, they sang a few carols, adding even more magic to the special night.

Finally, when everything was ready, the toys lined up in a row, waiting for Santa Claus to arrive. As the clock struck midnight, the fireplace suddenly glowed with a red light, and Santa stepped into the room with a big smile on his face.

"Ah, I see that my favorite toys have not let me down again!" Santa said, looking at the beautifully prepared presents and the wonderfully decorated tree. "Thank you, my little friends. None of this would be possible without you!"

Sarah gave a curtsy, and Charles beamed proudly. "It's our honor, Santa!" said the plush bear. "We want to make sure that every child who receives us has the most magical Christmas ever."

Santa looked at each of the toys with gratitude and said, "Remember, what you do makes a huge difference. Every little joy you bring to children makes the world a better place."

With those words, Santa bid farewell to the toys and hopped into his sleigh to continue his

Christmas journey. The toys watched him take off, waving goodbye, and felt that they had truly added to the magic of Christmas.

As dawn approached and the children began to wake, the toys returned to their places, pretending nothing had happened. But they all knew that on that night, they had created something truly special together.

From that day on, every Christmas was filled with magic, and the toys knew that they had their own little part in bringing joy to all the children.

The Little Bear's First Christmas

In the middle of a dense, snowy forest, where the trees stood covered in a blanket of white, lived a little bear named Thomas. Thomas was a very young bear, and this was going to be his very first Christmas. He had never experienced this magical moment before, and though he felt excited, he didn't quite understand what Christmas was all about.

One day, while Thomas was strolling through the forest, he came across his friends—Squirrel Nancy, Fox Michael, and Deer Betty. They were all busy preparing for the upcoming holiday, decorating a small Christmas tree in a clearing. Nancy was hanging nuts and dried fruits, while Michael was placing little red berries on the branches.

"Hi, Thomas!" called Nancy with a big smile. "Are you ready for your first Christmas?"

Thomas looked at them uncertainly. "I'm not sure what it's all about," he said, shaking his head. "What makes Christmas so special?"

Betty came up to him and gently placed her hoof on his shoulder. "Christmas is a time when we share with others and give presents, but it's not just about things. It's about being together, enjoying each other's company, and spending time with friends and family."

"And the magic!" added Michael, jumping up with excitement. "On Christmas Eve, amazing things happen that you can't explain. It's a time when even the smallest gestures can make someone feel happy."

Thomas felt his heart swell with warmth and joy. "I'd like to share something special, too," he said with a smile. "But I don't have anything to give."

"That's not true, Thomas," said Nancy, handing him a small apple. "The most important thing about giving gifts is the heart you put into them. You don't need to have much, just share what you have."

Thomas took the apple and decided to give it to Deer Betty, one of his best friends. When he handed her the apple, Betty looked at him with gratitude. "Thank you, Thomas," she said warmly.

"It's not the apple but the thought and care that matters most."

At that moment, the first snow began to fall on the clearing. White snowflakes danced in the air, adding magic to the scene, and all the animals looked up, enchanted by the beauty of the winter scenery. Thomas felt his heart fill with joy and realized that Christmas was about more than just presents—it was about sharing love, warmth, and friendship.

As evening came, everyone gathered around the Christmas tree in the clearing, and Nancy lit the tiny lights that twinkled like stars in the sky. The animals started singing carols, and laughter echoed throughout the forest.

Thomas sat next to his friends, gazing at the tree and the glow of the lights. "This is truly the most beautiful evening," he said with a smile. "I never knew Christmas could be so magical."

Nancy wrapped her little paws around him. "Christmas is special, Thomas, because we spend it together," she said. "It's not about what we get but what we give and how we share our hearts with others."

Thomas looked at his friends and knew that although this was his first Christmas, it certainly wouldn't be his last. He understood that the true magic of the holiday wasn't in the gifts but in love, friendship, and being together.

And so, surrounded by his friends in the warm glow of the Christmas tree, little Thomas experienced his first, most wonderful Christmas, filled with joy, love, and the holiday spirit that he would remember forever.

Printed in Dunstable, United Kingdom